Glasgow Victoriana

Classic Photographs by Thomas Annan

Introduction and captions by James McCarroll

First published in the United Kingdom by:
Fort Publishing Ltd, 12 Robsland Avenue, Ayr, KA7 2RW. Telephone 01292-880693.

ISBN 0 9536576 0 4

Designed by:
Paul McLaughlin, 48 Queen Street, Lochmaben, Dumfries, DG11 1PS.

Printed by:
Cordfall Ltd, Glasgow.

All photographs courtesy of the Mitchell Library, Glasgow, with exception of page 64 and back cover. Special thanks to the staff of the Mitchell Library.

Front cover:
Glasgow Bridge and the Harbour
(see page 37)

Title page:
Head of High Street

St Vincent Street Church, designed by the great Glasgow architect, Alexander "Greek" Thomson and built between 1857–59. The church is still in use today as a place of worship.

Introduction

The City

At a certain point in the life of a city, a number of factors conspire to thrust greatness upon it. So it was with Victorian Glasgow. All the necessary elements were in place: cheap and plentiful coal and iron ore; technological innovation; a highly developed banking system; worldwide demand for capital goods; growth in trade with North America; the widening and deepening of the Clyde; the availability of labour.

During the lifetime of Thomas Annan, the city of Glasgow was transformed into an industrial powerhouse: the Second City of Empire. Its entrepreneurs were known throughout the world: Sir William Burrell in shipping; Lord Kelvin in electrical engineering; Sir Thomas Lipton in retailing; Robert Napier in shipbuilding; William Beardmore in heavy engineering; Sir Charles Tennant in chemicals. The word "Clydebuilt" became synonymous with quality as its factories and shipyards led the world in productivity and innovation. In these years, it was calculated that Glasgow produced upwards of one-fifth of the world's ships.

As great fortunes were made, the men behind them built lavish houses and public buildings to advertise their wealth. The sheer scale of the new architecture was to make Glasgow, in the eyes of many, the most impressive Victorian city in the world. Great architects such as Alexander "Greek" Thomson, George Gilbert Scott and Charles Wilson gave the city an architectural legacy second to none. Glasgow's civic pride was eloquently expressed by the opulence of the City Chambers in George Square. In the west of the city, elegant terraces were planned to accommodate a burgeoning and self-confident middle class.

Victorian Glasgow did not neglect its pleasures while engaged in the pursuit of wealth. Great parks and open spaces were laid out. The West End (now Kelvingrove) Park opened in 1853, the Queen's Park in 1862 and Alexandra Park in 1870. New entertainments in theatre, music hall, and professional football were welcome diversions from the world of work, while Glasgow's new shops were amongst the finest in Europe.

Yet despite the undoubted self-confidence of Glasgow's bourgeoisie, and the dynamism of its economy, there is another side to the story. While contrasts between the Victorian rich and poor are now a historical cliché, they were nowhere more pronounced than in Glasgow. Central to the city's problems was the sheer number of newcomers, as the population increased from 200,000 in 1831 to 500,000 in 1881, reaching almost 800,000 by 1901. A further difficulty was that the physical contours of the Clyde Valley meant useable housing land was in short supply. As a result, Glasgow's working classes were packed tightly into a central core. Indeed , by the turn of the century, 700,000 people were living in an area which measured only three square miles, with densities of 1000 people per-acre commonplace. Glasgow had become the most heavily-populated urban-centre in Europe.

To maximise the limited space, Glasgow became a city of tenements. The classic Glasgow tenement was a four-storey building, accessed by a public corridor or close serving a number of individual dwellings. Large numbers of the tenements were "single-ends": one-room properties with bed recesses or box beds. The sanitary arrangements were primitive, consisting mainly of shared earth-closets in the backcourt. In many cases, a solitary tap in the close was the only water supply for a four, or six, storey tenement. Overcrowding on this scale, along with the complete lack of sanitary facilities, inevitably had dire consequences for Glasgow's health. Epidemics of cholera, typhus and smallpox haunted the city throughout the nineteenth century. Tuberculosis, a child of overcrowding and inadequate diet, was another scourge.

However, it was Glasgow's good fortune that the energy of its merchant class was matched by the vigorous response of the civic authorities. Glasgow was at the forefront of new developments in municipal provision and public health. In 1859, despite the fierce opposition of vested interests, the Glasgow Water Works scheme at Loch Katrine was completed. While, in 1863, the first Medical Officer—Dr Willliam T. Gairdner (pictured on page 54)—was appointed. Gairdner and his successor, the legendary James Burn Russell, helped bring higher standards in sanitation, food hygiene and in the control of infectious diseases. Recognising the crucial importance of good housing, the municipal authority also embarked on a programme of slum clearance through the Glasgow City Improvement Trust, and commissioned a certain Thomas Annan to make a photographic record of the properties it intended to demolish.

Thomas Annan

The Man

Thomas Annan was born in the village of Dairsie, Fife in 1829, the fifth of seven children of John Annan and Agnes Bell. His father was a farmer and flax-spinner. Following four years as an apprentice to a lithographer in the Fife town of Cupar, Annan arrived in Glasgow to work for Joseph Swan, a well-known engraver and lithographer. Annan soon developed a keen interest in a new form: photography. In 1855, he established his own photographic business in Woodlands Road, and in 1857 moved to more fashionable premises in Sauchiehall Street. Due to the success of these ventures he was able, only two years later, to open a photographic printing works in Hamilton.

In his early career, Annan forged a reputation as a photographer of works of art and he was justifiably recognised as an outstanding technician. One of his best-known works was a photograph in 1865 of the huge painting, Signing of the Deed of Demission, a highly complex and challenging commission by the standards of the time. The painting was the work of the great Scottish artist and photographer, David Octavius Hill, who was not only a close friend and admirer, but also a great influence on Annan.

He covered a wide range other material. Portraits of famous Glaswegians. Postcards of Firth of Clyde holiday resorts. Glasgow streetscapes. The grand houses of the Glasgow gentry. The ceremonial removal of the professors of Glasgow University from the old buildings in High Street to a new campus in the west end of the city. Reflecting his strong religious beliefs, a set of photographs of the painted windows of Glasgow Cathedral. Annan was also drawn to the countryside and won acclaim for his depiction of rural scenes in photographs such as Lochranza and the Last Stooks of Harvest. Many of these photographs were published in book form at the time, usually with a commentary written by a co-author. Perhaps the best known of these publications are *Photographs of Glasgow with descriptive letterpress* by the Rev. A.G. Forbes, (published in 1868); *The Old Country Houses of the Old Glasgow Gentry* (1870); *Memorials of the Old College of Glasgow* (1871).

Despite the brilliance of this work, Annan's fame rests largely on his series, "The Old Closes and Streets of Glasgow". This was commissioned by the Trustees of the Glasgow Improvement Scheme, which intended to demolish the city's worst tenements as a precursor to providing better quality housing for the working classes. However, before the clearances began, and all traces of the old closes disappeared, the Trustees had the foresight to engage Annan to make a photographic record. Published in three editions between 1868 and 1900, they are without doubt some of the most historically significant photographs ever taken.

At his death in 1887, the obituarists concentrated on Annan's achievements as a photographic innovator, artist and entrepreneur: he was responsible for the advancement of photography not only as an aesthetic form, but also as a technical process, and introduced several new techniques to Scotland, including photogravure. Much was also made of his skills as a copier of works of art. However despite the lack of recognition from his contemporaries for his role in recording social conditions, he is remembered today primarily as a chronicler of the rapid change which swept through Glasgow for much of the nineteenth century. It was central to Annan's genius that he was able clearly to record the very different faces of Glasgow, moving easily from the gilded world of the great industrialists to the slum areas occupied by their less privileged fellow-citizens.

The Old Closes and Streets of Glasgow

It is a stroke of great historical fortune that Annan was commissioned by the Glasgow City Improvement Trust to make a photographic record of the soon to be demolished slums. He was not only a painstaking photographer with an unerring eye for detail, but also a genuine innovator, and the photographs on the following pages are an eloquent testament to his talent.

Taken between 1868–71, the "Old Closes" series constitutes the first comprehensive view of slum life. The series also vividly captures a Glasgow which has now completely disappeared: many of the buildings dated from the seventeenth century, and some were older still. While we do not regret the passing of the slums many fine buildings, such as the Tontine Hotel in the Trongate, have also been lost.

Annan's work in Glasgow places him alongside the other great chroniclers of slum life in the late nineteenth-century. These include Jacob Riis, whose photographs of the New York poor were the catalyst for social reform, and John Thompson, who movingly recorded the lives of the London poor. While Annan had no grand political or socio-economic motives, his views of the closes are genuinely moving and full of pathos. They reveal the horrific living conditions endured by tens of thousands of Glaswegians in the

Close no. 75 the High Street, 1868

midst of one of the world's most economically vibrant cities.

At least three editions of the series were published between 1871 and 1900, with a different set of photographs in each edition. The 1900 edition included some photographs taken after Annan's death in 1887 (possibly by his son). In view of their historical importance, and for the sake of continuity, a number have also been reproduced here.

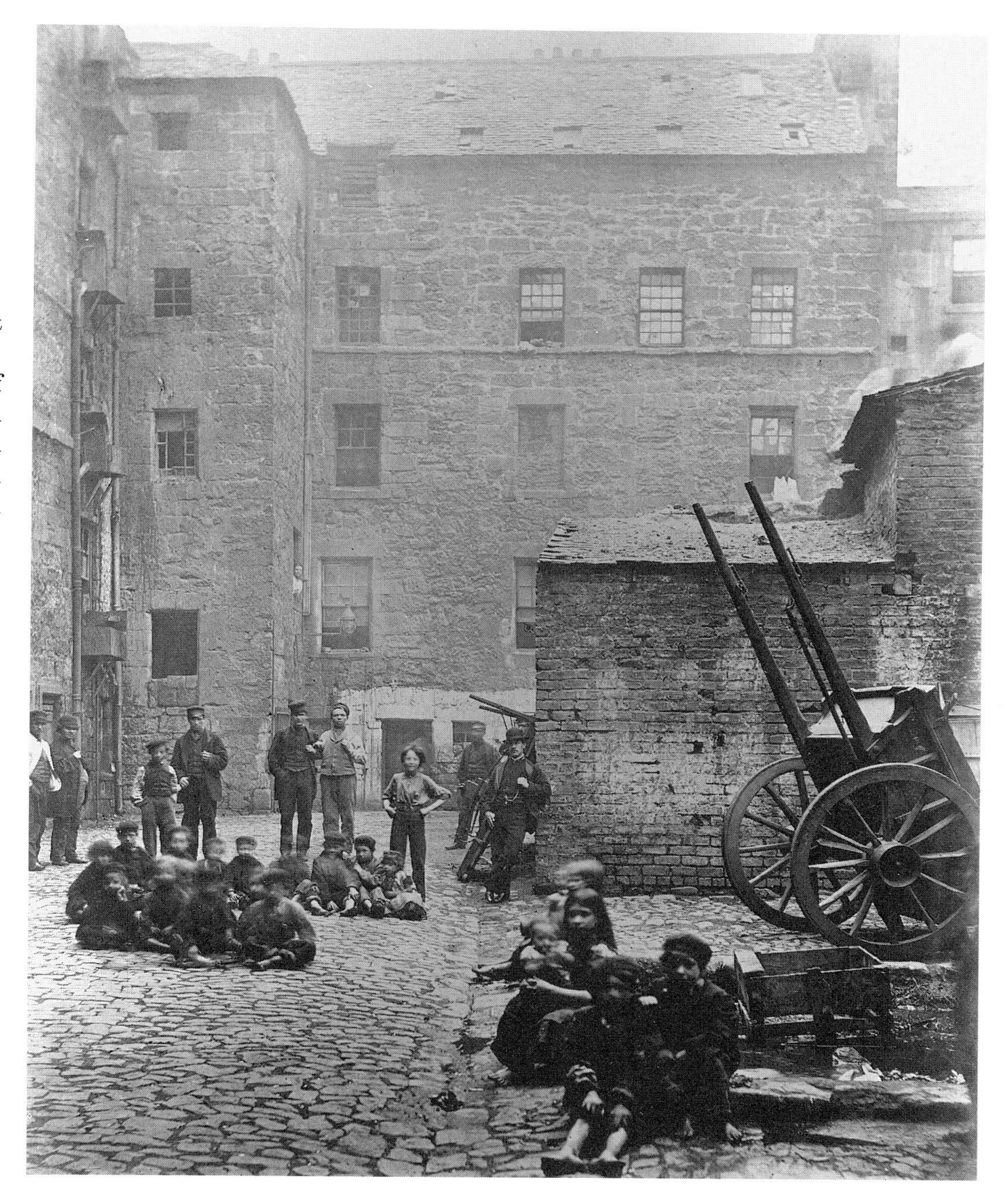

Close no. 46 Saltmarket, 1868

Close no. 28 Saltmarket, 1868

Closes nos. 97 and 103 Saltmarket, 1868

The Old Closes and Streets of Glasgow

Close no. 65 the High Street, 1868

The Old Closes and Streets of Glasgow

Close no. 37 the High Street, 1868

The Old Closes and Streets of Glasgow

Close no. 118 the High Street, 1868

Close no. 80 the High Street, 1868

The Old Vennel off the High Street, 1868

The Old Closes and Streets of Glasgow

Broad Close, No. 167 the High Street, 1868

Opposite:
Close no. 267 the High Street, 1897

The corner of Duke Street and the High Street, 1897

Opposite:
The Back Wynd, 1899

Close no. 11 Bridgegate, 1897

Opposite:
The High Street from College Open, 1868

The High Street from the Cross, 1868

Old Buildings, the High Street 1868

Main Street, the Gorbals, looking north

ENERAL RAG & METAL STORE
FROST &
TIMBER YA
J.O.B

Opposite:
Main Street, the Gorbals, looking south

Gallowgate 1868

Elphinstone Tower, Main Street, the Gorbals, 1868

Princes Street from King Street, 1868

Saltmarket from Bridgegate, 1868

King Street, City, 1868

Bell Street from the High Street, 1868

The Trongate from the Tron Steeple, 1868

The Tontine Building, Trongate, 1868

Bridgegate from the corner of Market Street, 1899

Saltmarket from London Street, 1885

Nelson Street, City, 1899

Annan around Glasgow

Annan took a range of fine photographs of his adopted city in the 1860s and 1870s. These included views of Glasgow's most elegant streets, and the grand houses of the city's leading citizens.

George Square, 1868
Glasgow's most famous square was named in honour of King George III. When first laid out in the 1780s, George Square was the exclusive preserve of the wealthy Glaswegians who owned the surrounding houses. Now, as in Annan's time, it is the city's best-known public space. The large statue in the centre is of Sir Walter Scott.

Glasgow Bridge and the Harbour, 1868
By nature a broad and shallow river, the deepening of the Clyde from the late eighteenth century onwards was central to Glasgow's development as a world industrial centre. By the time Annan took this photograph from the Old Sailor's Home in the late 1860s, the harbour was accessible to ships of more than 1000 tons.

Glasgow Cathedral, 1868
A sacred Christian site since the fourth century AD, the present building dates from the twelfth century. It is arguably the finest example of Gothic architecture in Scotland. The Necropolis, with its ornate tombs and mausoleums, can be seen in the right background.

West End Park, 1868
The Victorians were enthusiastic cultivators of public parks and, as in so many areas, Glasgow was in the vanguard. Work on the West End (now Kelvingrove) Park began in 1852, based on a design by Sir Joseph Paxton. It was later host to Glasgow's three great exhibitions, in 1888, 1901 and 1911.

Royal Exchange, 1868
This magnificent building, originally a private residence, was converted in the late 1820s to a commercial centre. The equestrian statue in the foreground, by Marochetti, is of the Duke of Wellington, and was erected in 1844. It is now the home of the Gallery of Modern Art.

Buchanan Street, 1868
Named after the tobacco merchant, Andrew Buchanan. Originally the location for the elegant residences of the rich it is now, as in Annan's time, Glasgow's most prominent shopping street.

Bridge Street and Carlton Place, 1870
On an otherwise deserted street,
a Hansom-cab can be seen plying
its trade.

Theatre Royal, Dunlop Street
There had been a theatre on this site since 1782, but the frontage shown in this photograph dates from 1863. The statues in the five niches include Shakespeare and Garrick. The building was demolished in the late 1860s to make way for a railway station.

City and County Building, Wilson Street
Designed by William Clarke and George Bell in 1842, this impressive Greek-revival structure was originally used as an administrative centre and for the Sheriff Court. Sadly, it is currently unoccupied.

Linthouse, Govan
Designed in 1791 by the great Scottish architect, Robert Adam, for the Spreull family. Adam was for many years the most prominent architect in England, but spent his last ten years in Scotland following a financially disastrous project in London. His output during this time includes Register House in Edinburgh and Culzean Castle near Ayr. The Linthouse, regrettably, was demolished in 1921.

Killermont on the Kelvin
Situated on the right bank of the River Kelvin, two miles north of Maryhill, Killermont House was built around 1805. It is a good example of Annan's interest in reflection (see also Dumbarton Castle on page 57). The house has now been demolished.

The Glasgow mansion house
The Glasgow mansion house was a regular feature of Annan's work, no doubt influenced by the lucrative fees which could be charged to wealthy owners. Regrettably, the location of this otherwise very interesting study is unknown.

Opposite:
Glasgow Cathedral
Annan's photograph affords an excellent view of the magnificent Gothic façade. On the left is Glasgow Royal Infirmary, built in 1792 to a design by the brothers Robert and James Adam. This magnificent Italianate building was demolished in 1912 to make way for the current Royal Infirmary.

Lansdowne Parish Church, 420 Great Western Road
This view of Great Western Road, taken in 1870, shows two bridges across the River Kelvin, both of which were demolished to make way for the present-day structure. The elegant church, designed by John Honeyman in the Gothic style, can be seen in the background.

Garscube House, around 1870
This fine house in the north-west of the city was designed by William Burn and built in 1827 for Sir Archibald Campbell. It was demolished in 1954 by its owners, the University of Glasgow, due to the presence of dry rot.

Memorials of the Old College of Glasgow, 1870

On 28th July 1870, the Senate of the University of Glasgow met for the last time in the Old College Buildings situated in Blackfriars, High Street. After more than 400 years on the same site, an elegant new campus had been built in the city's fashionable west-end. Annan was commissioned to produce a book of photographs to "secure some permanent memorial of the venerable structure".

The Old College buildings, designed by John Mylne, represent some of the most outstanding examples of seventeenth-century architecture in Scotland, and their demolition to make way for a railway goods-yard was a cultural disaster.

Principal doorway of College

The Hunterian Museum
The name commemorates the eminent surgeon, William Hunter who, at his death in 1783, left £8000 to Glasgow University to build a museum. The result was the splendid Old Hunterian Museum by the Dunfermline-born architect, William Stark. It was demolished with the other old University buildings in the High Street.

The College from College Street
A splendid view of the Old College, with academics on the left and their less prosperous fellow citizens on the right.

Dr Thomas Barclay,
Principal of Glasgow University, 1857–73.
Dr Barclay, a native of Unst in the extreme north of Shetland, supervised the transfer to the new buildings at Gilmorehill.

Sir William T Gairdner,
Professor of the Practice of Medicine from 1862–1900
Gairdner was appointed Glasgow's first Medical Officer of Health in 1863. He was a leading light in the campaigns to improve the city's housing and sanitary standards.

The exodus from the Old College
The professors, in full sub-fusc, leave the Old College for the last time.

The High Street façade
This view affords an excellent perspective of the old University buildings. A cab can be seen outside the principal doorway.

Annan at Large

Annan made frequent forays outside Glasgow, and produced work of great interest.

Dumbarton Castle
Annan's award-winning study clearly illustrates the strategic advantages enjoyed by this important castle. The site, a fortress since the fifth century, has been the scene of many fierce battles. William Wallace was imprisoned in its dungeons, and Mary Queen of Scots stayed for five months before sailing to France.

Lochranza, Island of Arran
This much-praised study captures Lochranza Castle, situated in the north of the island. The castle is still standing.

Millport, Cumbrae Islands
Annan took many photographs of "doon-the-watter" resorts on the Firth of Clyde. This view of Millport is a particularly fine example.

Dairsie Parish Church, Dairsie, Fife, 1860
This is a view of the parish church in Annan's home village of Dairsie. The church was built in 1621 by John Spottiswoode, Archbishop of St Andrews, and is considered a very distinguished building. It has an octagonal bell-turret and dwarf-spire.

Coltness House, Wishaw
A large, handsome edifice, Coltness House had a picture gallery nearly two hundred feet long. At the time of Annan's photograph, it was owned by the Houldsworth family, major landowners in Lanarkshire. The house has now been demolished.

The Last Stooks of Harvest
Another of Annan's highly-praised compositions, taken around 1860.

Loch Katrine: with water committee and commissioners, 1876
The Loch Katrine works, near Callander in the Trossachs, had been designed to provide Glaswegians with a wholesome supply of water. The scheme was completed in 1859. The loch's previous claim to fame derived from Sir Walter Scott who drew inspiration from its rugged beauty in his poem, The Lady of the Lake. The works are still in operation today.

Dr David Livingstone
Annan and Livingstone were neighbours and close friends. This study of the great explorer, taken in 1864, illustrates Annan's facility in portraiture.